Daddy Issues

By
Anna Krauze

Published by Playdead Press 2022

© Anna Krauze 2022

Anna Krauze has asserted her rights under the Copyright, Design and Patents Act, 1988, to be identified as the author of this work.

A CIP catalogue record for this book is available from the British Library.

ISBN 978-1-915533-01-2

Caution
All rights whatsoever in this play are strictly reserved and application for performance should be sought through the author before rehearsals begin. No performance may be given unless a license has been obtained.

This book is sold subject to the condition that it shall not by way of trade or otherwise, be lent, resold, hired out, or otherwise circulated without the publisher's prior consent in any form of binding or cover other than that in which it is published and without a similar condition including this condition being imposed on the subsequent purchaser.

Playdead Press
www.playdeadpress.com

Daddy Issues was first performed at the Camden Fringe Festival 2021 with the following cast and creative team:

Natalia (Nat)	**Anna Krauze**

Voice-over Cast

German Man	**Joseph Prestwich**
Family Voicemail	**Emmy Happisburgh / Harry Strudwick**
Marcus	**Joshua Ford**
Emma	**Emmy Happisburgh**
Peter	**James Gladdon**
Final Caller	**Ryan Wilson**

Creative

Writer	**Anna Krauze**
Director	**Coral Tarran**
Script Editor	**Sam Williams**
Producer	**Anna Krauze**

Cover design by Maria Krauze
Oil paintings & sketches by Anna Krauze

Daddy issues was supported using public funding by the Arts Council England.

PASSING STRANGER THEATRE COMPANY

ABOUT PASSING STRANGER THEATRE COMPANY

Passing Stranger Theatre Company was formed in 2018. We are focused on creating bold, thought-provoking shows that leave our audiences questioning their views and opinions. Our first production, a translation of a Polish, Shakespeare-like play, *Balladina*, was supported by the Polish Cultural Institute and the Polish Radio.

ABOUT DADDY ISSUES

Daddy Issues premiered at the Camden Fringe Festival 2021, followed by two national tours (Autumn 2021, Spring 2022), visiting theatres in Bristol, Kingston-Upon-Thames, Brighton, Glasgow and Nottingham. *Daddy Issues* was supported using public funding by the Arts Council England: we have been awarded the Arts Council National Lottery Project Grant 2021.

We performed *Daddy Issues* as part of the Omnibus Theatre's Summer Season of Edinburgh Previous (July 2022) before moving to the Pleasance Courtyard, 3-29th August 2022, for the Edinburgh Festival Fringe 2022.

Daddy Issues is currently being developed for a limited series TV script.

ANNA KRAUZE is a Polish-born actor, writer and producer. Anna is the founder of the Passing Stranger Theatre Company. *Daddy Issues* is her playwriting debut.

CORAL TARRAN is the director of *Daddy Issues*. She is also an actor and founding member/director of Mischief Theatre and one of the creators of their Olivier Award nominated show, *Lights, Camera Improvise!*

REVIEWS

"The play is driven entirely by Nat, a young Polish immigrant, and a phenomenal storyteller. Definitely has the potential to be a show talked about for years to come."
Theatre 503

"It is a bold and courageous bit of storytelling."
Channel 4

"Krauze has written a very deep and complicated character."
London Theatre 1

"Krauze's script is witty, comical and, most importantly, it's real. There are some genius moments in this one woman show and such a contemporary commentary on female sexual pleasure."
Everything Theatre

"Krauze is a talented storyteller with an original voice."
View From The Outside

To my Mami and my twin sister

Natalia, the main character. Playing age 25-35. She is a Polish immigrant, speaks with a strong Polish accent, but the play can be adapted to fit other nationalities as well. Nat uses other accents when speaking with her clients: British, American, Russian and German. Some of these accents can be replaced by other ones to suit the actor's abilities.

Natalia is a painter and there's artwork in the show – three large oil/acrylic canvases, as well as multiple drawings and sketches on the floor and on the walls. An actor can also sketch during the performance, but the artwork, especially the large paintings, can be created by another artist beforehand.

While the audience is seated, an automatic voice recording can be heard.

VOICE: Welcome to Daddy Issues. Please remember that our line is strictly regulated by certain rules: no underage, rape or murder experiences. No offensive behaviour tolerated unless it's mutually agreed as being part of the experience. Thank you for your understanding. We will now connect you with one of our girls. Please hold.

Hold music. Lights up.

Room in a small flat. Blow up armchair. Old fashioned phone with a very long cable is seen placed on a small table. Two easels with painting turned with their back to the audience. There are sketches and drawings on the walls and floor. We can see a pair of legs hanging over the armchair. A voice is heard, sounding like moans of pleasure. After a few moments Nat emerges from behind.

NAT: (*strong Polish accent*) Fuck's sake.

Puts the phone down.

NAT: I swear you get more and more demanding every day – Right, sorry…

(*Knowingly looks at the audience*)

I wouldn't want to make assumptions about you. I meant to say that MY CLIENTS get demanding –

Nat points at the phone she is using.

NAT: Try to keep up… People call me Nat now, short for Natalia here - but I go by many names – I can be Tanya, I can be Kate, I can be Lady bloody Madonna – anything you want. It's the stories that keep you coming back to me.

Phone rings.

NAT: (*in American accent*) No request too BIG or too small… What is it that you are looking for?

(*towards the audience, Polish accent*)

>Sounds too easy, ay? They like that. They don't want you to be smart. What do they want? Well. They want you to be just about of legal age, act underage and sound like a schoolgirl fascinated by anything they say... Who is willing to act however they please... As far as the phone conversation allows, that is.

(*Back to the phone in an American accent.*)

> What am I wearing?

(*Looks at the audience in disgust, mouthing 'Obviously.'*)

> My sporty clothes, silly... I'm wearing a tiny, little crop-top, which is very, very tight... And I'm wearing blue shorts... and they're really short because I've had them since 6th grade and my legs are so much longer now... I'm in...

(*Looks at the audience for their reaction.*)

> 11th grade now... Too old? Ah. Well. I just wanted you to think of me as a grown-up Daddy... I'm really only in 9th grade now. Yes, that's right, that does make me...
>
> (*winces*) Fourteen. Yeah. Mhmm. I just came back from a training sesh –

(Runs in a spot, panting.)

> I am really, really hot. And I'm sweating... Uh-huh. Yeah... Yeah, I'm sweating so much that my clothes are wet... so wet you can kinda see through them...
>
> (*giggles*) Yeah. Yeah that's right, I guess I'm kinda wet all over. Yeah. I do run a lot... Yes, I am used to being wet... Well, I am part of the running team... so my body is really, really muscular, and tight.

Nat hangs up.

NAT: (*Polish accent*) It's part of the appeal to the callers – the stories. They give you something unexpected. Sometimes you have a bad day and want a release. Sometimes you want to simply have fun without feeling awkward about your needs. Sometimes you feel lonely and want someone to talk to.

(*pause*) Sometimes you really anger me. Sometimes I want to know more about you. You carry a centuries-old baggage of toxic masculinity and society expectations, that shit can get heavy and you need a distraction. We all deserve to have an outlet to be playful.

>   A space where our kinks and desires are understood and explored without judgment. Not many of us are lucky enough to have that.

Beat.

>   The devil's in the details with you. You can't see me after all, so it's my job to make you feel something. You know when you binge on a really good TV show? You can't stop watching it! It's like that, but I put you in the middle of it. I'm serving you the cliff-hangers to make sure you're desperate to see the next episode.

(*Puts on a baby-girl voice.*)

>   Call me soon, Daddy… My heating is broken, it's so cold that my nipples are piercing through the t-shirt. Will you come tomorrow and assess the situation? I miss you already! I'm juicy just thinking about speaking with you again. I can almost feel your tongue between my thighs.

(pause)

>   And pragmatically speaking, I just try to keep you on the line as long as I can without being called out on that to

>   ensure my pay is right. I really like
>   having money.

Pauses in thought. Walks towards an easel facing away from the audience.

NAT: It's not something I'm used to, frankly - having cash. I studied in Poland. Gdansk Academy of Fine Arts, painting faculty - which I enjoyed even though I've been told way too often I try to be 'too edgy'. After graduation I scraped the last of my money for a one-way ticket and came here. I rented one of these disgusting, tiny rooms in East London, painted by day and worked in a souvlaki restaurant by night. I've organised a few exhibitions, there was one on Brick Lane which attracted an art collector called Peter. 'What a success,' you'd say, right? Nope. He said my art was a bit too disturbing to his taste and doesn't go well with Matisse.

(*pause*)

> Well, maybe I can please a daddy, but apparently, I am not capable of pleasing a rich gay man.

(*Turns the easel towards the audience. It's a close-up painting of a vulva with some menstrual blood.*)

Even though sometimes I get commissioned to paint a dick or two, my reviews said I'm aggressively feminist and clearly after men's blood. I mean, really? Men's blood?

(Shrugs.)

I needed the money if I was ever going to try and make it here. So I joined the Daddy Issues line to make it work. Because, boy oh boy, do I have stories!

Pauses. Looks at the audience.

NAT: I don't tell all these stories on my behalf, don't worry. It's good if we have our own tales to tell clients, sure - but we can borrow them from our mates too. Has your classmate been touched up by a handsy teacher in a changing room and liked it? Has your best friend's dad had a habit of getting drunk and overexcited about early teens at family birthday parties?

(Defensively, with a hint of sarcasm.)

Honestly? I have friends. With issues. And if you have been raised by at least one fucked-up, absent or, in fact – wholesome, decent parent who gives you unreasonable expectations, chances are you're in the club, even if you live in denial. Welcome to the world of Daddy Issues, darling. The gift that keeps on giving... So, call me, yeah?

Music. Working Bitch by Ashnikko.

Nat puts a flat cap on, sits on the armchair with her legs spread like men on the tube often do. She puts on a male voice in an English accent and gestures slowly.

NAT: (*as the Englishman*) I have been lonely, dear. Misunderstood. I am a journalist. I used to cover stories on the war in Iraq and now I barely cover any headlines. Day after day I'm stuck in a dark cubicle, copy-pasting press releases. My wife has no interest in me, she mostly avoids me. My daughter has moved out, still lives in London, but only comes to visit every so often – She's followed in my footsteps, went into journalism... She sometimes brings her friend – Milly – home to browse through her old teenage stuff. Milly is... lovely. Really, really lovely.

(*Englishman – Nat smiles to himself.*)

She asks a lot of questions about my job, she seems to look up to me, which is nice... Flattering even.

Takes a cap off, picks up the phone.

NAT: Uhm, Milly...

(*towards the audience*)

> The therapy bit. It comes once every ten calls or so. They usually sheepishly request...

Puts a cap back on, moves phone's head away.

NAT: (as the Englishman) Could you... Could you be Milly for a bit?

Music. Invitation by Ashnikko.

Nat bounces on a chair to enhance the fake moans.

NAT: (*In a Russian accent.*) You're a naughty, naughty boy, Mr Vasiliev...

(*Puts the phone to her heart, speaks towards the audience in Polish accent. Still bouncing.*)

> We become who the clients want us to be. We don't have to be perfect as long as we sell an illusion. He knows I'm not Russian, sure, but as long as I throw in a few '*zdravstvuytes*' and '*do svidaniyas*' in there, he is happy.

(*Into the phone.*)

> What is that, Mr Vasiliev?

(*Pause.*)

> What is my real daddy like? Oh, he is my favourite type of daddy!

(*To the audience, with a wink*)

> Absent, of course!

(*Back on the line.*)

> Yes, YES, you can call me Sashka, Mr Vasiliev. It is your daughter's name? How lovely. You are… You are shouting your own daughter's name now, oh – Okay… You would fuck Sashka if she would allow it… Yes, Mr Vasiliev, I've heard that one before… Mostly from politicians.

Hangs up.

NAT: (*own accent*) Oh, don't look at me like that, alright? I am simply living up to my national stereotype just as it is expected of me, an Eastern European sex worker. I need a plumbing job for the mornings and I will turn into a human embodiment of my country, drinking vodka and smoking fags all day shouting "*kurwa mać*" on every sentence. It'd be much easier than dealing with employers who never

	believe I have an actual degree and yell at me upon our first encounter…

(*Imitating English speakers talking to foreigners.*)

	'Your English is so good! Well done!'
(*Own voice.*)	
	Some older men often say that to me when they want me to fuck them. They never seem to understand that being patronised makes my pussy implode.
Beat.	
NAT:	There was this one man who understood that about me, how I hate being patronised. I still dream of him - of his strong hands lifting me up, his movements showing desperation to touch every part of my body, he's wanting… NEEDING me and my youth, my enthusiasm, my frivolousness. I am an adventure, I'm an unknown land, I'm a wet fucking daydream and an ego boost. And I enjoy it, every bit of it.
(*pause*)	
	He was a successful painter and the first man to put his hand around my throat. He had a wife, and two perfect

children. Ridiculously unhappy. He wanted an affair so bad. He couldn't stand his wife, but he was able to keep her away with a healthy cheque. He's hired me as his PA, I was doing all the boring stuff he couldn't be bothered with. You can probably guess how quickly it turned into doing all the naughty stuff instead. Yes, it sounds like a cliché, but it didn't feel like one. Because he never underestimated me. He said he loved my mind, he actually listened to my advice. I left some of my best work at his studio, haven't got it back yet.

Beat.

NAT: Huh. He still paints my body to this day... I know because I recognise my scars and my tits anywhere. But here's the thing with artsy daddies, once they realise they can TALK to you, like REALLY talk about their craft and FEELINGS... they fall in love with you. But of course... they don't want that. Because the reason they are in love with you is because you are fun and free of responsibility, and if they start to feel responsibility towards you, you are just another responsibility along with the wife and the kids and the car and the mortgage and the career – and what is sexy about that? So I ended it. Before he could. Nobody wants an affair to turn serious.

Sits down with a sigh.

The problem with affairs with these older men who want to be in charge – is that we keep them a secret as if ashamed, because they don't go well with our feminist agenda. But honestly? We have to admit that sometimes we simply want to be pushed against the wall and…

(*Starts moaning like during a great orgasm.*)

Ohh… Ahh…

Beat.

NAT: We want both tenderness and roughness. Domination and submission. Being kissed and being sucked, made love to and being fucked. Older men get that, they can sometimes read female desires better than we do ourselves. You don't often get that from boys who get their knowledge of female anatomy from PornHub. Boys are ignorant, they don't want to listen to our bodies. Come

on, learning sex from porn is like
learning life from soap opera TV… Stop
thinking it's real. And ask your Dad for
tips, boys. Daddy knows best.

(*Looks towards the sky, she does that to refer to someone else than the audience.*)

Oh God. Fuck off. I didn't mean you…

(*Hinting it's her father, she speaks to the audience.*)

I meant you. I hope you're taking notes.

Nat's mobile phone rings. Nat picks up, a little surprised. She's used to the tone of the landline.

NAT: Nat…alia speaking. Hi, yes. How do you have my num… Oh, leaflets, exhibition – of course. Menstrual vagina? That's me. You are…? A journalist. A podcast, okay. You… Want to ask about my paintings? And why do I paint vaginas? Well, technically they're vulvas not vaginas… But men often confuse the two, don't worry. Anyway…

(*Smiles to herself.*)

A more experienced artist once told me to paint what I know, so… Yeah. Uhm. Yes, I have modelled for myself, initially. Later on, I started painting some of my more...

(*Sits on the armchair, spreads her legs.*)

OPEN friends, you know what I mean? Europeans mainly. We tend to be a bit more relaxed about nudity than the Brits.

(*pauses*)

Dicks are drawn from cultural memory. It starts at school, before we know how they work, we learn how to draw them. And mama, we draw them – all over our pals' notebooks and foreheads, we wallpaper toilet walls with cocks in full detail, veins and drips and all. It took me quite a few attempts and hours of awkwardly bending over mirrors to paint my vulva correctly. But dicks? We get dicks fed for breakfast. They slide uninvited into our DMs.

(*Mockingly.*)

"Hey, baby. Nice smile." Dick. "U wanna?"

(*Puts the journalist on speaker.*)

We learn to please the dick before we learn to please ourselves. We know more about giving a good head, men have no issue with grabbing our heads and thrusting to teach us how it's done. We are happy to please them, yet we feel ashamed of touching ourselves down there. We want to be all courageous in describing what we want but end up sending our sex partners youtube videos explaining fingering on tropical fruits. Dicks are majestic. Teenagers know that. Gen Z boys describe their female pals as having "a big-dick energy". Vulvas are the ugly embarrassment of body parts. It's men who dictate what they should look like to make them 'prettier': less hairy, porn perfect, 'baby smooth'. BABY smooth? Who the fuck decided this should be a phrase? 'I like when a woman feels baby smooth down there'. Mate, if that's what you're into I'm way too old for you and I am twenty years your junior. How fucked up is that? Baby smooth. And God forbid we ask for orgasms in return. Nice girls don't do that. You can give cheeky blow jobs in club toilets, it's okay to be a little whore then, but don't be a slut at home, don't talk orgasms, honey. For real now, can women even have them?

(*Pause. She realizes she went off on a tangent*)

> And it is why I turn to vulvas. Very passionate about the subject, yeah. Anyway, this...

(*Gesticulates a conversation.*)

> Is this for your podcast then? Oh, and Instagram... Sure, I consent, whatever. Yes, for the 'gram too.

Noise of the caller hanging up.

> I dread the thought that online fame is where careers peak these days. It terrifies me, you know? Here's me, trying to tell intimate stories of women only to get opinions given in likes.

She turns another easel with a painting of legs spread open.

> Someone commenting on one of my vulvas: "Nice cunt! I would".

(*Gesticulates an emoji in the air.*)

> Aubergine emoji. Aubergine emoji. Aubergine emoji. Highlighting the enthusiasm.

(*pause*)

> I worry about being forgotten. Don't you? Seriously, it's a perpetual fear of

mine. I'm planning another exhibition to avoid dying as a Little Miss Nobody, a depressed artist wannabe with a decent amount of social following mainly consisting of middle-aged men sending me snaps of their downstairs. It doesn't fucking matter. The likes, not the downstairs, that matters sometimes. Point being, if everyone's an artist, does it mean that nobody truly is one anymore? You're never good enough, influential enough, you always do too little, create too slow for the demand. Still, I paint, snap pictures of my art and upload it online, because that's just what you do these days to get noticed. Then, people say you're only as good as your last review…

(*Pauses.*)

"Nice cunt! I would."

(*Gesticulates the emoji three times.*)

The landline phone rings. Nat ignores it.

Music. Manners by Ashnikko.

Quick furniture reshuffle.

NAT: (*Stands with her back to the audience.*) Look, I have a theory that it's a plan of

bad daddies to release as many
daughters with issues into the universe
as possible. Is that what you were
doing, Daddy? Is that what I am?

(*Looks up. Ponders sadly for a moment, before remembering she's being watched. She shakes off the vulnerability.*)

A sperm-fuelled legacy for future
generations, so their thirst for broken,
father-needing women is always
fulfilled?

Turns around.

NAT: (*sarcastically*) Sounds like a lot of
responsibility to me. But it needs to be
done, these vulnerable women need to
be out there for the modern Daddy
seeking invigorating romance with
youngsters. The strategy of an affair is
tricky enough as it is! He may never
know which girl may be lying about her
age or accuse him of sexual harassment
– hashtag MeToo. He can never be
certain. It's hard – being scared of
living out your sexual fantasies –
especially if you have – God forbid – a
reputation to lose! And, you know – a
family to hide it from. But who cares
about those?

(*pause*)

You can tell when a man is hiding something. He becomes meticulous about small things, he's nicer to you and he smells of pure soap. Never trust a man who smells strongly of soap. He is washing the blood from his hands.

Beat.

I did have a long-term boyfriend once. We broke up over a year ago. We used to laugh a lot and say silly things to each other. I would say: 'I worry that when I'm a successful painter, someone will break into my PornHub account and publish my search history'. And he would say absurd things. You know... 'Babes, I would never hurt you'.

(*pause*)

I came back home early one day because I was unwell and the smell of souvlaki made me feel sick. I found him in our bed with a girl. I had a bag of takeaway souvlaki with me that I brought for him. I stood there, watching her get dressed, mumbling something under her breath. As she passed, I pushed the doggie bag into her hand like some good Samaritan – I didn't know what else to do with it. She grabbed it, a little shocked, and wrapped her arms around me awkwardly. I stood there like a proper cold bitch...

(*She smiles slowly.*)

And then I fucked her father.

(*Looks up. Pretends to feel ashamed.*)

What? Too much? Fine, I haven't fucked her dad.

(*To the audience. Winks.*)

I totally fucked her dad.

Beat.

So it was the girl that I took it out on... Not on my cheating boyfriend, but her. I use other women to explain what men have done to me all my life to convince myself that it's got everything to do with her and nothing to do with what's wrong with me. Which, there is, I'm not saying...

(*Looks up.*)

Don't.

(*To the audience.*)

> We do that – women. I can't be the only one. Wanting her to be the bitch.
>
> Still, I can't stop thinking...
>
> I wish I'd have fucked his dad instead.

Landline rings. Music – Little Boy by Ashnikko.

NAT: (*As Lisa, in American accent.*) No issue too big or too small, what is it that you're looking for? Hello, Adam... Oh, what's your surname again? It sounds very important, like a Lord! Nice to hear such a mature voice, Adam. I adore English accent. You can call me Lisa. What brings you to me?

(*Grabs her mobile, looks something up while keeping the conversation going.*)

> Uh-huh. Yeah... You want to dominate me? Oh, I don't know about that, Daddy. I have never even seen a penis IRL...

(*Towards the audience in her own accent. Still glances at her mobile occasionally.*)

> Clients do this more often than you think, introducing themselves by their full name as if they were calling their doctor. They get a little awkward after letting it slip, so I try to make them feel

comfortable while googling them immediately. LinkedIn, company website, painting the picture of their working life. An office? But what kind? Is he a lawyer, a dentist or a graphic designer? Instagram, Facebook, do they use these? I'm excavating their personal lives to tailor my performance. You name it, I use it. I'm an expert in the craft by now.

(*Investigates her phone.*)

Adam is middle-aged, often wearing socks with sandals. Ironically! He's also a Scorpio… A life coach who enjoys preaching to young women about body positivity and being woke. I wonder if he coaches his clients to practice domination on sex lines to improve their own lives.

(*To the phone, in American accent. Sounding slightly scared.*)

I will obey my Daddy now and be a good little girl, I promise. I'm Pisces after all. Please, be gentle with me.

Music. Gorąca Prośba by Chylińska. Part 1.

NAT: (*To the audience. Hiding frustration.*) I sometimes do get satisfaction from happy clients on my phones. A job well done. I'm really good at it now. But this is not why I'm here. I'm a painter and I want my art noticed.

Today my works were featured on the ArtReview, which is incredible, right? Only... they had already seen them. I emailed them to the London editor a while back and invited them to come see my stuff in Shoreditch. They wouldn't review it then. Too explicit, they told me. So how come they reviewed them now? New editor? A change in taste? No. They reviewed my works now because they think they're by Marcus Trent.

Beat.

Trent is actually someone I used to know... Closely. That's what I thought at least. I think I mentioned him to you. He was furious when I ended things. Threatened to hurt himself. We fell out big time. He kept a bunch of paintings I stored at his place out of spite. I figured out it was petty revenge. Thought I'll have them back for my next exhibition. But no. Turned out he sold them and made a fortune, passing them off as his own. They went for twenty-five thousand British

>   pounds a piece, following the review.
>   He didn't need luck, he just needed to
>   be a dude. Well fucking done, Marcus.

(*pause*)

>   The review said his work was raw and
>   intimate. An admiration of complex
>   female emotions. Marcus said in the
>   interview that memories of his sexual
>   encounters have made his brush move
>   on the canvas almost all by itself,
>   guiding him through the creative
>   process... He didn't mention however
>   that his female admiration peaks when
>   he chokes them.

Music. Hit me baby one more time by Britney Spears.

Landline rings.

GERMAN MAN: (*German accent*) Papa's home, baby.

NAT: (*Responds in a German accent to please him, but you can tell her heart is not in this.*) Hey, Papa. I've been waiting for you for SO LONG... I hope you are going to make it up to me...

GERMAN MAN: Were you a good girl? Did you go to bed by 11 like you promised? Did you hope your Papa would come in to kiss you goodnight?

NAT: Oh, mein Vater. I was praying every evening it would happen. I tried to be so good, but I can't promise I was behaving all that well...

GERMAN MAN: That makes me quite unhappy. You bad girl, I will have to punish you.

NAT: (*Getting into it, provocatively placing fingers in her mouth.*) Vater, bitte. Please don't. It's not my fault all these boys want to slip their fingers inside of me.

GERMAN MAN: (*strongly, in German*) Ruhig, mein Kind. Du wirst hören, was Papa Dir sagt. Daddy knows best how to handle you.

Nat's breath intensifies. She slowly, awkwardly puts her hand in her pants to check what she fears for, she discovers she's wet. She rapidly hangs up the phone. Nat freezes for a moment.

NAT: (*Polish accent. Awkwardly.*) Right. That does happen.

(*Towards audience.*)

I wish that wanting older men was only a thing for women who adore their dads and as an adult find no one lived up to their expectations - that at least makes sense. They just sit on someone else's lap instead.

(*Empty laughter.*)

> But what if you have an absolute shit-show of a father? We ought to be independent man-eaters out for revenge. That would be socially acceptable. So why the hell do we find ourselves up searching for daddy porn at 2am?

Music. Grey and Lilac by Lola Young.

(*Picks up her mobile phone, dials. Waits.*)

FEMALE VOICE: You've reached Jessica, Marcus, Jack and Will's home phone! Sorry we missed your call. Please leave a message after the tone and we'll get back to you as soon as we can.

Loud beep.

NAT: Pick up, you asshole. I know you can hear me. I know you're awake because of your insomnia. I can see you… sitting at your enormous kitchen table with a glass of overpriced whiskey, smoking under-priced fags, like every night we've spent together. Pick up, you fucking coward. Have you read what's been said online, how everything I did to date was a fraud? That I've been stealing from you for years. Just what the British public expect from a foreigner, eh? It was clever of you to play into that. Looks like I'm finished and it's by your curious hand.

A phone is picked up.

MARCUS: Hello? Nat? Natalia? Natalia please, hear me out. Please. I had to do this. I had no choice. I have the house, my studio... I have Jack and Will for God's sake, boarding school fees cost a fortune. Natalia... I've been... I've been trying to kick the coke habit – you know how hard I tried, but I cannot focus, cannot fucking paint these days and Jess wouldn't understand... You know she never did... That's why you were so precious to me... you really... you listened. I felt heard with you. I felt safe. I think actually I could have gotten clean if only you'd stuck around...

NAT: Don't you fucking dare.

MARCUS: Nat, I needed this for my family, my career. You don't even have a career, darling. If what we had together ever meant anything to you, you will let this go. You know how much I loved your art, to be honest you can see my input

	in it, I helped you evolve... Really, you can't prove any of this, Nat, so it's best for both of us if you drop it.
NAT:	Drop it, huh? Have you forgotten about the texts you used to send me? About my work. About us. Must have slipped your mind that I don't have a 'Jess' to hide and delete messages from. The public would think I've forged them, you've got me there. But your wife will know they came from you. She will know it's your dick on my phone. Next time it will be her I'd get in touch with. I bet she would love to know her husband she's called a psycho for wanting to choke her has found a keen bitch after all. I doubt she will make it easy for you to see the kids after that. So don't fuck with me.
MARCUS:	You... You wouldn't. You are nothing without me.
NAT:	You've got some fucking nerve. Go fuck yourself, Marcus.

Hangs up. Music. Gorąca Prośba by Chylińska, Part 2.

Landline rings. Nat doesn't pick up. She lies flat on the floor staring at the ceiling.

NAT: (*Looking towards the ceiling.*) I've considered OnlyFans, but I find it overpopulated. It's just another social media app, only more... openly sexy, unlike the fakely prudish Instagram. I've lost my exhibition after the industry called me a thief of the renowned artist's work. So I considered finding a sugar daddy as another way of expanding my sex network now that my painting career is dead and buried. You wouldn't approve of this sorta thing for your own daughter, but I know you would love another girl her age to jump your bones. Daddy's have double standards.

(*Looks at the audience knowingly.*)

So, I went to the website, set up a profile. I think I was curious and a little desperate. That attracts them like bitch. My photo wasn't even that good, but I got three offers pronto, one guy asking for a close up of my feet. You have options to choose from, dates, dinners, travel, sex. Most of them treat you like charity work or a good deed for a day.

(*pause*)

I agreed to meet 'Richard' in a cafe. I saw him through a window with cappuccino foam on his massive moustache, slowly licking his lips like the psychopaths in crime drama. I ran away and that was the end of it. At least on the sex line they're unable to murder me and I could pretend they all look like Leo DiCaprio. Classic dad body and I would still fuck the life out of him.

There's music in the background throughout this entire scene – Numb by Portishead.

Nat has her art, drawings, paintings, spread on the floor. She pours paint from the bottles onto them, covering and destroying her works. She slowly rips the paper, covering herself in paint while doing so. Nat's mobile phone rings. Nat picks up, surprised at its tone. She can hear two voices on loud speaker. The first is male, posh and camp. Another – female, calm and professional. The woman speaks before Nat has a chance to say anything.

FEMALE CALLER: Is that Natalia Kaczmarska? Hi, my name is Emma Langley of Langley Associates, I'm here with an art collector, Peter Klein. He's seen your work before, we've searched for you and listened to a podcast interview, the one where you spoke a lot about…

NAT: (*Speaks with a tone of sarcasm.*) Dicks. Yes, I mean, yes, it's me. Speaking.

FEMALE CALLER: I've been keeping an eye on your vulva paintings. I find them interesting. Honest and quite emotional, actually.

NAT: I don't know. Maybe. Sometimes I'd try and suggest the mood of a person with the shades... Anyway, it's not important. I'm done with it.

FEMALE CALLER: I know why you say that. I saw uncannily similar art to yours in a recent review of a famous painter. Would you like to tell me what happened?

NAT: Are you asking if I was the one stealing from Marcus Trent? Is that it?

(*Laughs sarcastically.*)

Where are you really calling from? Daily Mail? You fucking love foreigners there.

MALE CALLER: Ouch. She bites. Look, you probably don't remember me, we spoke only briefly at your Shoreditch exhibit. I was looking to buy some art. I didn't, but your style made an impression.

	Cunts, cunts, cunts, I thought – lovely. Not my usual go to… But I've thought about your paintings a lot.
NAT:	They surely don't go well with Matisse.
MALE CALLER:	You remember.
NAT:	I remember a lot. It is usually more of a curse than a blessing.
FEMALE CALLER:	We think you deserve another chance. You see, I know Trent stole from you. I know him… closely. He isn't a first-time fraud, he was involved in something…
(*bitterly*)	
	Very similar when we were in art school together. He's gotten away with it. Listen, I've contacted the ArtReview. You may expect a rectification from them.
NAT:	I am kind of grateful, but it also looks like you are calling me because of this scandal and how using my name could get you some press.
MALE CALLER:	You're a bit of a cynic, love, aren't you?
NAT:	The world – it gets darker in my head.

MALE CALLER: You're sharp, darling. I like it.

NAT: You're wasting your time. I'm done trying to be an artist. He wins. The internet doesn't forget names being dragged through shit. Instagram said I deserved it all for trying to get famous off the back of someone established, called me a slut too because that seems to be relevant somehow. Twitter said that my interviews "confirm I despise all men". I'm not... I'm just done. I'm really fucking done.

FEMALE CALLER: I won't force you to do anything, Natalia. But I can assure you, he hasn't won yet. Not unless you let him.

MALE CALLER: We are working on a project. A few of our painters are commissioning a collection of self-portraits, interpretation of an artist in the modern world. We want it to be honest, raw. I have a feeling you could have a lot to say.

FEMALE CALLER: You can think of it as your chance to take control of the narrative again. Tell your side of the story and show you are a bolder, stronger painter than Trent, I know you can do that. You see, what

	feels like defeat can be a chance for rebirth. Give it some thought?
NAT:	And I don't have to sleep with you?
FEMALE CALLER:	(*on a smile*) Sleep on it instead. Okay? You've got my number.

The callers hang up. Nat sits there puzzled.

The landline rings.

NAT:	H-hello?
CALLER:	(*Harsh, deep male voice*) You can't stop thinking about me.
NAT:	Who… Who is this?
CALLER:	You're my daughter. You've missed me. You thought you would never see me again. But after many years I'm back and you are so grateful. Tell me how grateful you are.
NAT:	(*getting angrier*) So FUCKING grateful.
CALLER:	(*forcefully*) No! You are a nice girl. You don't swear, you don't use that tone. Not with your Daddy, not with anyone, but especially not with Daddy. Do you understand?

Natalia freezes, breathing angrily, but says nothing.

CALLER: (*Cont'd. Slowly*) Good. Good. You're getting there. I finally found you. You're a grown-up young woman now. Look at you, you thought you could leave the past in the past, but you were not able to fill this void. And now I'm back. Years of absence, but you couldn't be happier. You want to hug me, to touch me, you've waited for this moment for so long. 'Daddy', you say. 'Daddy, you really are here'.

His breathing speeds up, excited. Nat's mouth turns thin and trembles angrily.

NAT: You, leaving has been a valuable life lesson. It taught me to trust no one, especially the likes of you. You taught me that love is abusive and cruel, something to run away from. I can't love healthily, not myself, not anyone. It's like the more I try, the worse it gets. You made me believe that everybody leaves and everybody lies. And somehow, you were right.

CALLER: (*breathing intensifies*) Yes. Yes, tell me what I taught you. Tell me what you've learned.

NAT: (*seriously*) You want to know what else I've learned, DADDY?

CALLER: Tell me, baby doll.

NAT: (*taking her time, angrily*) Your daughter is better off without you, you piece of shit.

Hangs up forcefully. She lets go of the phone's head but starts to slowly wrap the cable around her wrists like handcuffs throughout the speech.

NAT: (*Looking up.*) Father. It's a big word, isn't it? A word never used lightly. Founding father. Father figure. Father Almighty.

(*pause*)

It's a word and a promise – of guidance and safety you replaced with terror. It's sleepless nights, waiting for you to come back. Hoping you won't be in the same state as the night before. Listening for whether she's okay after you've raised your hand again. There's a sound of breaking glass. There was so much broken glass.

(*Gleefully, like a child.*)

The mornings are quiet. Almost blissful, blink and you'll miss it. You are asleep, you won't be able to go to work which means you won't drink as much tonight. Maybe I will sleep a little better, it makes it easier to wake up for school. School is okay. I'm very good at hiding! I win every fucking emotional game of hide and seek. Then I come home and we do it all again.

Beat.

I never asked you for anything, never once begged you to stay. It's simple, really. I just didn't want to feel... fucking invisible.

(*pause*)

I can't shake off the shame of you. It has grown into my bones and tattooed itself onto my skin. I pray at night to exorcise your ghost, I hope it won't come back to haunt me at dawn.

Beat.

It always does. Eventually. I sometimes think I've forgotten about you only to find you in the actions of men I desperately want to trust. I feel broken, lonely, unlovable. Avoiding commitment, then committing too much, wanting another human to help me find my worth, because I don't know where to look for it anymore.

>   Using lovers to fill the void but feeling emptier each morning. Looking for a safe place in the arms of older men. After all, doesn't daddy know best? That's what we're taught.

(Empty laugh.)

>   You suck me into the black hole of you, just like you did with mom. Have you ever thought of that? How isolated and small you've made her feel, how desperate to quiet her head that her only way out was to swallow a handful of pills… Slip away almost unnoticed. Fuck knows where you were. So many homes and legs welcomed you, that I lost count.

Beat.

>   I didn't want to end like her. I needed to protect myself from you… I just didn't know how. That is why when I'd come back and found you there, your vomit Jackson fucking Pollocked across the kitchen floor, I hesitated, DAD – because it was Christmas day – but I called the goddamn ambulance…

(Beat.)

>   Just a bit too late.

Laughs coldly, exhausted. Takes a moment before speaking again.

> Nobody teaches you how to protect yourself from your own family. How to raise above what you have witnessed all your life. You need to figure it out while still being the one called a crazy bitch. How did 'Daddy Issues' become a way of insulting women - when it's about how men have failed as fathers?

Nat's wrists are now properly tied with the cable. She begins untangling it as she speaks, to finally put it down.

> I blame myself for denying you help. Am I a monster here? You're long gone and I cannot direct my anger at you anymore. I cannot sit you down, a grown woman speaking to an older man, and tell you that I understand more now. You were an arsehole, but maybe you weren't taught any better yourself. Maybe it's a cruel generation game. Maybe you were not strong enough... I am stronger than you. Because every day I have to try and learn to forgive myself for what I've done. Does it ever get easier? Can I forgive you, for my own sake? The last thing I told you was that I would never

speak to you again, but here I am. Saying goodbye.

Fade.

There's a new painting in the middle of the stage – a naked body, hands trying to reach her, but she is out of touch. New exhibition, maybe? Nat gathers her props, placing them in a box. She moves to unplug the cable when the phone rings. She doesn't pick up.

NAT: (*using an 'educated' Polish accent instead of a strong, 'simple' one she used throughout.*) I can become who I want to be. I can be Lisa, I can be Sashka, I can be Natalia. Anything I want.

Phone rings again.

It's my story that keeps you coming back to me.

Nat does not pick up. The phone stops ringing. She bends to pick up first the box of props, then looks at the phone for a longer while, considering. Something comes to her, slowly. She smiles, places her set of keys next to the phone, leaving the set behind. She grabs her new painting, gives one final look towards her "father", the audience and exits the stage.

Beat.

Phone rings. Blackout.

Music – Daddy Cool by Boney M. CURTAIN.